AF528529

PREFACE

Welcome to the ultimate resource for mastering your IGNOU BCA Business Communication Previous Year Unsolved Papers BCS 055. Our collection of previous year unsolved question papers. This invaluable tool offers a unique opportunity to explore the types of questions that have shaped past exams, providing a window into the examiners' minds and the format you'll encounter. These unsolved papers are more than just a compilation of old questions; they are your chance to engage deeply with the subject matter and test your knowledge against real exam scenarios. Each paper challenges you to apply what you've learned in a practical context, helping you refine your skills and boost your confidence.

Dive into these papers to identify key topics, understand the exam's rhythm, and gauge your readiness. Use them to practice, strategize, and ultimately, excel. With diligent preparation and these insights, you'll be well-equipped to turn exam challenges into opportunities for success.

Table of Contents

BACHELOR OF COMPUTER APPLICATION
Chapter 1: Term-End Examination, December, 2013
BCS-055: BUSINESS COMMUNICATION

Time: 2 Hours **Maximum Marks:** 50

Note:

- Answer all questions.

1. Read the following passage and answer the questions given below: (10)

For starters, good negotiators find out everything they possibly can about the people they are negotiating with—what makes them tick, what they value, how they perceive the issue at hand. Money is usually a proxy for other deeper needs, and negotiations become easier once these needs are out in the open. "People fight over money because they don't know enough about each other," says Diamond. "Most people won't easily tell you their needs, but you have to persist in asking. You need to do research on every aspect of the individual. How long does it take for him to commute to work? How close is he to retirement? In the end, you need to see the pictures in their heads. It's more important to persuade them than anything you say or propose, including facts or expertise."

In the absence of specific information, people often go by stereotypes, taking guesses about what those on the other side of the table want. Diamond, who has done a fair amount of research on the subject of identity, says these biases can hurt negotiations: "Assuming things about the other person because he or she is American, Islamic, an attorney, a woman or the employee of a certain company is too imprecise. Our research found most successful women don't get their identities from being women—they get it from many other things. You should focus on each individual and how they view things at the moment of the negotiation," he says. Though people may feel more comfortable negotiating with those from a similar background, there is actually more to be gained if there is diversity at the negotiating table. "Differences are the source of profitability," says Diamond. "Work groups in which people disagree produce three times as many marketable ideas than consensus groups. Homogeneity is less profitable."

Still, when diversity at the negotiating table is high and people make insufficient efforts to understand each other, there is a danger of things becoming confrontational. Despite everything, threats and coercion remain common tools in negotiations, leading to conflict and communication breakdowns. When threatened, people become angry, irrational and indifferent to self-harm. "They focus from the solution to the threat itself. People lose sight of the goals and just want to retaliate. It becomes extremely personal," says Diamond.

Another destructive strategy often used by negotiators is to walk away from the table, which is probably the worst kind of threat. "Walking away sends a signal that you don't care enough to even talk to the other party. The alternatives are usually war, litigation or no deal."

The more important the negotiation is, the more emotional people tend to be. In such situations, the logic of facts and figures counts for very little. If a negotiator finds himself losing his calm, Diamond advises him to exit the negotiation and bring someone else. "If you become emotional, you lose," he says. "On the other hand, you have to be prepared to handle the emotional issues of the other party—empathize, apologize, listen to them, give them something they like. Otherwise, they are not persuadable."

Answer the following questions:

(a) What do you think should be the title of the passage? Give reasons for your answer. (2)

(b) What does a negotiator need to know for a successful negotiation? Discuss. (2)

(c) "In the absence of specific information, people often go by stereotypes..."
Discuss this statement in the light of the passage. (2)

(d) Threats are also sometimes used in the negotiation process. What are the consequences? List them

(2)

(e) When should a negotiator leave the table? And why?

(2)

2. Vocabulary from the passage:

(10)

(a) Find words from the text that mean the same as the following words/phrases:

(5)

(i) Prejudices

(1)

(ii) The ability to share someone else's feelings by imagining what it would be like to be in their situation

(1)

(iii) Generally accepted decision among a group of people

(1)

(iv) An act of forcefully persuading someone to do something that they are unwilling to do

(1)

(v) To hurt someone because they have done/said something harmful to you

(1)

(b) Find words from the reading passage which mean the opposite to the following words/phrases:

(5)

(i) Give up

(1)

(ii) Loss

(1)

(iii) Heterogeneity

(1)

(iv) Solution

(1)

(v) Peace

(1)

3. Grammar: Fill in the blanks

(10)

(a) Fill in the blanks with the correct forms of the verbs in brackets:

(5)

(i) I am sure we ***(meet)*** our targets if we ***(maintain)*** our current level of sales.
(ii) If I ***(be)*** in your position, I ***(insist)*** on having more staff in the department.
(iii) I ***(meet)*** an old business colleague of mine while I was travelling to Delhi for a conference.
(b) Fill in the blanks with a/an, the, or no article:

(5)

Sanwa Bank, one of ___ world's largest banks, is offering its clients. Savings account for ___ pets. Client's pets can hold accounts where they can save for special treats, holidays, or visits to ___ vet.

4. Write short notes on any two of the following:

(10)

(a) Importance of a Portfolio in an interview
(b) Features of a Business Proposal
(c) An Effective Group Discussion
(d) Guidelines for writing e-mails

5. Letter Writing:

(10)

Imagine that you work in a company's public relations department. An American company has written asking for some information about your company. Draft a short letter briefly summarizing your company's structure and the product(s) it deals with.

BACHELOR OF COMPUTER APPLICATION
Chapter 2: Term-End Examination, June, 2014
BCS-055: BUSINESS COMMUNICATION

Time: 2 Hours **Maximum Marks:** 50

Note: Answer all the questions.

1. Read the following passage and answer the questions given after it: (10)

For many years after independence, language policy had largely been held hostage by the perception of the English language as a 'colonial relic.' However, English is no longer a British tongue - it is more the language of international business, and a powerful key in opening up geographical borders and gaining access to markets. It is the language of science and research, with 90 per cent of papers across scientific journals written in English. It dominates the chatter of the Information Age - 80 per cent of the worldwide web is in the English language. It has been estimated that within a decade half the world's population will have some skill in English.

A commitment towards learning English was part of China's bid to host the Olympic Games, to the point that taxi drivers who failed an English test did not have their licences renewed and hotlines were set up to report incorrect English use in public spaces. Most countries are fast recognizing English's role as a world language, and besides China, nations such as Japan, South Korea, and Indonesia are including English as a compulsory language in their schools and setting up 'English-immersion camps' for students.

India has an advantage in the global market in the depth and breadth of its English-language capability. Today, Indians have embraced the idea of English as the language of the globalizing Indian economy. Most middle-class Indians speak in at least two tongues - besides their mother tongue, they have at least functional fluency in English for business purposes and to manage communication with different communities. Over the last fifty years, English has grown deeper roots in the Indian community, beyond purely economic value. Its reach has spread - to print, film, television, and ordinary conversation. English has rapidly become the language of creative discourse - and while Indian writers writing in English have remarked that they often face hecklers at their readings who demand to know why they do not write in their mother tongue, such criticism has become marginal in recent years.

Answer the following questions:

(a) Is English still considered a 'colonial relic'? Discuss. (2)

(b) Discuss the status of English in the contemporary world. (3)

(c) Can English be considered an Indian language? Discuss. (3)

(d) Give a suitable title to the passage. Give reason(s) for your answer. (2)

2. Vocabulary from the passage: (10)

(a) Find words from the passage which mean the same as the following: (5)

(i) A belief or opinion held by many people and based on appearances.

(ii) A system/tradition from the past which has survived and continues to exist.

(iii) People making loud unfriendly statements/questions.

(iv) Opportunity to enter.

(v) Treated as unimportant.

(b) Pick out words from the passage which are opposite to the following words/phrases: (5)

(i) Weak

(ii) Excluding

(iii) Rejected

(iv) Local

(v) Praise

3. Complete the following passage: **(10)**

(a) Complete the passage by supplying the correct prepositions: (5)

There is a man I do not care very much __, an engineer __ the name __ Barlow. He has been __ leave for quite a while.

(b) Complete the passage by correctly inserting *a* or *the*: (5)

While I was walking along __ main road the other day, I happened to notice __ small brown leather purse lying on __ pavement. I picked it up and opened it to see if I could find out __ owner's name.

4. Write short notes on any two of the following: **(10)**

(a) 'STAR Structure'

(b) Walk-in interviews

(c) The importance of social 'small talk' in business

(d) Different styles of communication

5. Write a profile of yourself: **(10)**

Your company has a new MD who has asked all employees to write a report describing their job profile so that they may be appropriately trained. Write a profile of yourself in 150 words.

BACHELOR OF COMPUTER APPLICATIONS
(Revised)
Chapter 3:Term-End Examination, December, 2014
BCS-055: BUSINESS COMMUNICATION

Time: 2 Hours **Maximum Marks:** 50

Note: Answer all questions.

1. Read the passage given below and answer the questions that follow: (10)

1. For many years after independence, language policy had largely been held hostage by the perception of the English language as a 'colonial relic'. However, English is no longer a British tongue — it is more the language of international business, and a powerful key in opening up geographical borders and gaining access to markets. It is the language of science and research, with 90 percent of papers across scientific journals written in English. It dominates the chatter of the Information Age — 80 percent of the worldwide web is in the English language. It has been estimated that within a decade half the world's population will have some skill in English. A commitment towards learning English was part of China's bid to host the Olympic Games, to the point that taxi drivers who failed an English test did not have their licenses renewed, and hotlines were set up to report incorrect English use in public spaces. Most countries are fast recognizing English's role as a world language, and besides China, nations such as Japan, South Korea, and Indonesia are including English as a compulsory language in their schools and setting up 'English-immersion camps' for students.

2. India has an advantage in the global market in the depth and breadth of its English-language capability. Today, Indians have embraced the idea of English as the language of the globalizing Indian economy. Most middle-class Indians speak in at least two tongues — besides their mother tongue, they have at least functional fluency in English for business purposes and to manage communication with different communities.

3. Over the last fifty years, English has grown deeper roots in the Indian community, beyond purely economic value. Its reach has spread — to print, film, television, and ordinary conversation. English has rapidly become the language of creative discourse — and while Indian writers writing in English have remarked that they often face hecklers at their readings who demand to know why they do not write in their mother tongue, such criticism has become marginal in recent years. These Indian writers, once called dissenters and mavericks, now include Amitav Ghosh, who have attained a status in English literature that has moved far beyond the exotic value of an Indian writing in the language.

Answer the following questions:

(a) Suggest an appropriate title to the passage and give your reasons for it. (2)

(b) What is meant by the term 'colonial relic'? (1)

(c) Explain the meaning of the phrase 'a powerful key in opening up geographical borders and gaining access to markets.' (2)

(d) Give instances from the passage which suggest that English is now an international language. (3)

(e) "English has grown deeper roots in the Indian community, beyond purely economic value." Discuss in the light of the passage. (2)

2. Vocabulary from the passage: (10)

(a) Find words/phrases from the passage which are similar in meaning to the following: (5)

(i) Notion (para 1)

(ii) An opportunity to enter (para 1)

(iii) People who pester and taunt (para 3)

(iv) Non-conformists (para 3)

(v) Alien (para 3)

(b) Find words from the passage which mean the opposite to the following words: (5)
(i) Local (para 1)
(ii) Optional (para 1)
(iii) Slowly (para 3)
(iv) Praise (para 3)
(v) Seminal (para 3)

3. Complete the following: (10)

(a) Complete the passage using the correct forms of the verbs and expressions in the box. You may change the tense of the verbs: (5)
1. Set aside money
2. Pay good interest
3.Have a budget
4. Got an allowance
5. Keep track of When Sunil was growing up, he _______ every week from his parents, and because he wanted to go to college, he _______ every month. He opened a savings account that _______, so his savings grew. In college, he didn't have much money, but he _______ and stuck to it. He _______ the money he spent, and when he bought things, he always paid in cash.

(b) Write questions for the answers given below. Use the question words in the brackets: (5)
(i) He works for the Perfect Health Magazine. (Which?)
(ii) He lives in Chennai. (Where?)
(iii) He goes out of town three or four times a month. (How often?)
(iv) He often meets important doctors. (Who?)
(v) He writes about preventive health. (What?)

4. Write short notes on any two of the following: (10)

(a) Some safe and unsafe topics for small talk
(b) Difference between a Portfolio and a Resume
(c) Features and uses of a Memo
(d) Different kinds of Reports

5. Write a letter of complaint: (10)

Your street is not being properly cleaned. Write a letter of complaint to the Health Officer of your area clearly stating:
1. The state of your street
2. Why it is not cleaned
3. When was it last cleaned
4. How to solve the problem

BACHELOR OF COMPUTER APPLICATIONS (BCA) (Revised)

Chapter 4:Term-End Examination, June, 2015

BCS-055: BUSINESS COMMUNICATION

Time: 2 Hours
Maximum Marks: 50
Note: Answer all questions.

1. Read the passage given and answer the questions after it: (10)

1. There is a point when a ripple turns into a tidal wave, a wind into a blizzard, and a movement into a revolution. The tipping point that truly transformed IT attitudes across the country was the rise of the telecom sector.

2. Since the 1999 telecom policy, the industry has grown exponentially, and teledensity growth has surged from 0.7 percent in 1991 to 27 percent in 2008. India's mobile network is gaining over eight million subscribers every month — its biggest problem right now is getting enough spectrum — and at the present rate, the country is set to soon become the world's second-largest telecom network.

3. This has been the transforming platform, which on top of our other layers of electronification is allowing us to try out multiple, mix-and-match IT-enabled infrastructure. It has, for example, enabled the banking network to integrate mobile and internet networks with automated banking. Meanwhile, an NSDL-led national Tax Information Network (TIN) is tying in India's direct tax systems with the IT platform of stock exchanges, the depository market, and banks. The network has helped the government dramatically expand the tax net and is a major factor for the rise in India's direct tax collections, which grew a record 40 percent in 2007–08.

4. The growing connections between the banking platform, the mobile phone platform, and the railway reservation platform are paving the way for services that, among others, allow consumers to book and pay for train tickets on their mobile phones. One of the fastest growing of such transactions today is the payment for airline tickets purchased over the internet with credit cards and mobile phones. Each time such a high-speed, telecom-enabled transaction replaces an 'old-economy', slow, paper-based one, we are seeing a productivity pop that ripples through the economy.

5. However, the lack of the most basic connectivity has deeply limited rural India's growth, since it cuts off access to critical information such as market prices for crops and weather patterns. Transmitting information about a price shock around a certain crop from the central markets to the outlying rural areas can sometimes take months. As a result, farmers in India find out about a price collapse too late, often after the planting season. For these farmers, IT is not just access to the information economy — it is their only access to it, and a critical, life-changing one.

Answer the following questions:

(a) Suggest a title to the passage and give reasons why you think it is appropriate. (2)
(b) 'Tipping point' in paragraph 1 means: (2)
(i) a point when a change becomes irreversible
(ii) an important point when change just begins
(iii) the bending point when a transformation happens
(c) What was the one factor which transformed the way we looked at the IT sector? Give one example. (2)
(d) Pick any four areas from the text, where IT has integrated with other services. (2)
(e) Why is IT access to farmers so important? Discuss. (2)

2. Vocabulary: (10)

(a) Find the words from the reading passage (in Q.1) which are similar in meaning to the following words/phrases: (5)
(i) Severe snowstorm
(ii) Rapidly

(iii) Completely changing
(iv) Bring together
(v) Crucial
(b) Find the words/phrases from the reading passage (in Q.1) which are opposite in meaning to the following words: (5)
(i) Fall (para 1)
(ii) Minor (para 3)
(iii) Decrease (para 3)
(iv) Urban (para 5)
(v) Extensive (para 5)

3. Grammar: **(10)**

(a) Complete the following sentences with the correct prepositions: (5)
(i) There was a steady increase ___ the sales of laptops.
(ii) There was a rise ___ 20% since last year's performance.
(iii) Prices of T.V. sets rose ___ ₹10,000 to ₹20,000.
(iv) Prices of T.V. sets went up ___ 20%.
(v) Inflation remained stable ___ 2-5%.
(b) Complete the following sentences using *must*, *mustn't*, or *needn't*: (5)
(i) I've to attend a meeting tomorrow, I ___ be late.
(ii) I haven't got any money left, I ___ go to the ATM.
(iii) We've got plenty of time, we ___ hurry.
(iv) These visitors are very important, we ___ find a good hotel for them.
(v) The restaurant is never full, we ___ book in advance.

4. Conversation & Writing: **(10)**

(a) Give a suitable response to each of the following introductions and greetings: (5)
(i) Pleased to meet you.
(ii) How's the family?
(iii) How are you?
(iv) It was very nice meeting you.
(v) Have a good trip back.
(b) Write a short note on any one of the following: (5)
(i) Need for a good Curriculum Vitae
(ii) Travelling for business

5. Memo Writing: (10)

Write a memo to your staff in which you state that your company is going through difficult times and you would welcome suggestions by the staff on austerity measures that the company could take. (You are the General Manager of the company)

BACHELOR OF COMPUTER APPLICATIONS (BCA) (Revised)

Chapter 5: Term-End Examination, December, 2015

BCS-055: BUSINESS COMMUNICATION

Time: 2 Hours
Maximum Marks: 50
Note: Answer all questions.

1. Read the following passage and answer the questions given after it: (10)

It is easy for writers to assume that readers are mirror-images of themselves, with matching interests and needs; but only in highly specialized writing is that often true. If you are writing for a high-level research journal, you can reasonably assume that other high-level researchers are much like you. But in most professional contexts, your readers will want to use the information to meet needs different from yours. In particular, in reports within industrial organizations, the amount of detail needed will vary considerably as information rises through the management hierarchy. In general, the higher the managerial level of your readers, the more their interests move from the technical how and why to the more commercial to what purpose and at what cost.

It is often helpful to sit and consider just what your reader will do after reading your paper: file it, reach for the phone, write a memorandum, sigh deeply, build some apparatus, write a cheque, arrange a meeting, sign an order, delegate someone to talk to you, re-use the information in an examination, or apologize to you? Such speculation is not an invasion of privacy! It is a necessary part of bringing exactly into focus the aim of the document. Many documents fail because writers have not thought enough or clearly about their aims. Many writers are content with vague ideas about the use of the document.

We are not saying that writers never consider their aims—just that they rarely consider them enough. Tactics must be based not on a half-conscious assumption, but on a detailed examination of the aims, which brings those aims fully into consciousness. We know of no better way of starting this process than visualizing what, specifically and physically, your reader will do with the document.

When you have an important paper to write, try to write yourself a short job specification—a few sentences outlining your objectives, audience, constraints, and possible procedures. This 'target statement' will help you cross the mental barrier between a lazy, half-formed idea, and a clear idea. As so often, the act of writing down an idea transforms it. Try writing a target statement for the next piece of writing you undertake.

Answer the following questions:

(i) Writers assume that "readers are mirror-images of themselves". What does this phrase mean?
In what sort of writing is this true? (2)
(ii) What kind of information do the managers who are higher up in the hierarchy prefer? (2)
(iii) Why do several pieces of writing fail? (2)
(iv) What is the author suggesting a writer should do if s/he has an important document to write? (2)
(v) Give a title to the passage. (2)
(b) Find words from the passage which mean the same as the following: (10)
(i) Differ (Paragraph 1)
(ii) A system of organization in which people have different ranks or positions depending on how important they are (Paragraph 1)
(iii) Pertaining to scientific and industrial topics (Paragraph 1)
(iv) Involving business (Paragraph 1)
(v) Give someone the duty of acting on your behalf (Paragraph 2)
(vi) Thinking about the possible effects of something (Paragraph 2)
(vii) Not clear (Paragraph 2)
(viii) Methods that are used in order to achieve what you want when you are dealing with other people (Paragraph 3)

(ix) Imagining what something is like by forming a mental picture of it (Paragraph 3)
(x) Something that limits or controls (Paragraph 4)

2. Fill in the blanks with *will*, *would*, *shall*, or *should*: (5)

(i) When my sister was three years old, she ___ tear the pages of my book.
(ii) Your jacket is torn. You ___ get it repaired.
(iii) The accountant has promised that he ___ disburse the salary tomorrow.
(iv) ___ you return my book as soon as possible?
(v) We ___ avoid telephoning anyone late in the night.

3. Complete the following sentences with the past or past perfect form of the verbs given in brackets: (5)

(i) There ___ (be) no one in the school at 4 pm. Everyone ___ (leave) by then.
(ii) I ___ (feel) very nervous in my first flight to Mumbai as I ___ (never, fly) before.
(iii) I ___ (can) not recognize my old classmate Rahul, he ___ (grow) very tall and fat.
(iv) Since I ___ (not, visit) my uncle for a long time, I ___ (feel) guilty.
(v) My son ___ (look) very happy when he ___ (see) the new puppy on the floor.

4. Write short notes on any two of the following: (10)

(i) Organizing a Portfolio
(ii) Group Discussions
(iii) Features of a Memo
(iv) Communication across Cultures

5. Write an e-mail: (10)

You are visiting a business associate in Singapore. S/he already knows about your visit. Write an e-mail to her/him giving information about your arrival date, day, and time. Request for a pick-up at the airport.

BACHELOR OF COMPUTER APPLICATIONS (BCA) (Revised)

Chapter 6: Term-End Examination, June, 2016

BCS-055: BUSINESS COMMUNICATION

Time: 2 Hours
Maximum Marks: 50

Note: Answer all questions.

1. Read the following passage and answer the questions given after it: (12)

Nowadays, audiences are used to seeing visual material during almost any sort of talk or presentation. Listening isn't easy, and it helps a great deal if you have something to look at; in any case, human beings tend to remember what they see more readily than what they hear, and so audiences are grateful for the reinforcement of a good visual aid. People also like looking at pictures — it makes a pleasant alternative to listening — and a change in the way in which information is presented adds variety and interest to the occasion and so helps them to concentrate.

For all these reasons, audiences want visual aids, and most speakers provide them. There are, no doubt, some highly experienced, witty, and knowledgeable people who can hold an audience's attention by themselves, but it's probably unwise to assume that either we or you are of their number.

If audiences are helped by visual aids, so are speakers themselves. Visual material is prepared in advance, and if it's well-designed and thoroughly checked, it becomes an area of the presentation that the speaker doesn't have to worry about, assuming, of course, that the equipment is available and functioning properly.

It also deflects attention from the speaker. This can be bad as well as good: it's possible to use so many visual aids that the audience feels they are seeing a film or video rather than meeting and listening to a human being. As films and videos can be transported easily from one place to another, they may also feel that it was rather a waste of their time bothering to come to the venue on a particular day at a prescribed time, when they could have watched the whole thing at home at their leisure. On the other hand, many speakers like to feel that occasionally during the talk they are not the main focus of the audience's attention; this is often true at the beginning, and is a good reason for having a visual aid containing the subject and the speaker's name to show as the presentation starts. It may also be helpful in allowing the audience to see how the speaker's name is spelled.

Answer the following questions:

(i) How does the audience benefit from the use of visual aids in a presentation? (2)
(ii) What kind of people can hold the audience's attention without visual aids? (2)
(iii) Why is it a good idea to use visual aids on the part of the presenter? (3)
(iv) Why is it necessary to have a visual right at the start of a presentation? (2)
(v) What are some of the disadvantages of using visual aids? (2)
(vi) Give an appropriate title to the passage. (2)

2. Vocabulary: (8)

Pick out words from the passage which mean the same as the following:
(i) Providing more evidence or support for an idea (Paragraph 1)
(ii) Something different from what you already have (Paragraph 1)
(iii) Amusing in a clever way (Paragraph 2)
(iv) Minutely (Paragraph 3)
(v) Take the attention away (Paragraph 3)
(vi) To take to some other place (Paragraph 3)
(vii) Place where an event is happening (Paragraph 3)
(viii) At your convenience (Paragraph 3)

3. Fill in the blanks with the linking words given in the box: (5)

even though, whereas, so, after, since
(i) The Guptas live far from the city centre, ___ they don't get many visitors.
(ii) ___ she had promised to visit them, she went there the next day.
(iii) The English eat potatoes, ___ the Chinese eat rice.
(iv) He went to bed ___ he had finished the book.
(v) My weeks in captivity weren't too terrible, ___the food was awful.

4. Fill in the blanks with the appropriate form of the verbs given in brackets: (5)

(i) The Principal ___ (have) finished his round of the school and is returning to his office.
(ii) As soon as Richard ___ (hear) the news on the radio, he rushed to the accident site.
(iii) The message ___ (arrive) after he ___ (leave) the office.
(iv) I ___ (think) of inviting all my close friends for dinner.

5. Write short notes on any two of the following: (10)

(i) Business events
(ii) Writing an effective proposal
(iii) Different styles of communication
(iv) What is a Portfolio?

6. Letter Writing: (10)

There is an advertisement for the recruitment of trainees in office management in your local newspaper. Write a letter of application, mentioning your organizational skills and educational background.

BACHELOR OF COMPUTER APPLICATIONS (BCA) (Revised)

Chapter 7: Term-End Examination, December, 2016

BCS-055: BUSINESS COMMUNICATION

Time: 2 Hours
Maximum Marks: 50

Note: Answer all questions.

1. Read the following passage and answer the questions given below: (12)

In my time at the company, I saw many such transformations. One was how the perception of IT changed rapidly across Indian industry — fifteen years ago, the chairman of a leading bank, the Union Bank of India, criticized my efforts to promote the benefits of bank computerization to the industry. Recently, however, his successor called me up and told me with pride that they were running the entire bank on one central computer system.

India has gained dramatically from similar, massive changes in our attitudes towards our population, entrepreneurs, the English language, globalization, and democracy. It has made India a country that right now has a unique cadence, where all our major strengths have come together and matured at the same time. There are countries around the world, for instance, which are at a demographic sweet spot but lack the democracy they need to exploit it. There are some nations that have huge natural resources but not the entrepreneurs and technologies to spread the wealth. And there are countries whose previous, unsuccessful experiences with globalization have scarred them so deeply that they shun it, and this limits how much they can gain from their domestic strength. In essence, I think no other country in the world right now has the combination that makes the Indian opportunity so significant.

We Indians have keenly felt both our humiliations and our successes. So the buzz surrounding our two and a half decades of growth has not been missed by any of us. Wherever I go, I find that Indians know our growth numbers backwards and forwards, and there is a strong, common feeling among us that our country has finally come of age. But it has not been an easy ride — the ideas that now bedrock India's economy took decades to be widely accepted and were often caught up in the storm of our politics and shifts in public opinion. In retrospect, each big part of the Indian miracle seems a little miraculous.

Answer the following questions:

(a) What do you think is the profession of the writer? (2)
(b) What are the reasons for India's significant gain, according to the writer? Give any four. (2)
(c) Name three things that can make a nation successful. (3)
(d) Describe the feelings that Indians have about their country. (2)
(e) Why did these "ideas" take so long to come to fruition? (2)

2. Vocabulary: (10)

(a) Find words from the passage which mean the same as the following: (5)
(i) Great changes (Paragraph 1)
(ii) People who begin a business (Paragraph 2)
(iii) Special (Paragraph 2)
(iv) Badly hurt (Paragraph 2)
(v) Feeling of being looked down upon (Paragraph 3)

(b) Find words from the passage which mean the opposite of the following: (5)
(i) Slowly (Paragraph 1)
(ii) Praised (Paragraph 1)
(iii) Lost (Paragraph 2)
(iv) Few (Paragraph 2)
(v) Ordinary (Paragraph 3)

3. Memo Writing: (10)

There is a recession in the country and your company wants to introduce austerity measures. Write a memo to the staff of your company, suggesting ways of economizing on the use of paper, electricity, and so on.

4. Write short notes on any two of the following topics: (10)

(a) Characteristics of a good formal letter

(b) Preparing for a job interview

(c) The importance of understanding different cultures

(d) Different styles of communication

5. Fill in the blanks: (5)

Complete each sentence with suitable forms of the verbs given in brackets.

Cars ___ (pollute) the air in the cities for many years. In addition to pollution, cars ___ (increase) the problem of congestion in crowded urban areas. A professor of medicine from an American University ___ (believe) that the automobiles ___ (be) responsible for a large number of heart attacks that Americans have because they ___ (not, walk) much anymore.

6. Make Wh-questions: (5)

Make Wh-questions with the following as shown in the example:

e.g.: Find out when Mr. Jain will be back.

Answer: When will Mr. Jain return?

(a) You want to know where the nearest chemist is.

(b) Find out when Mr. Joseph normally arrives at the office.

(c) Find out what the mobile number of the Managing Director is.

(d) Find out how she spells her name.

(e) You want to know why the consignment has been delayed.

BACHELOR OF COMPUTER APPLICATIONS (BCA) (Revised)

Chapter 8: Term-End Examination, June, 2017

BCS-055: BUSINESS COMMUNICATION

Time: 2 Hours
Maximum Marks: 50
Note:
Answer all questions.
There are five questions.

1. Read the following passage and answer the questions given below: (12)

1. Looking back, the common man and woman have been bit players in our histories, their role determined by statistics and crowds. It is only recently, particularly since the 1970s, with the rise of labour productivity and the knowledge economy, that the political power of people has been accompanied by greater economic power.

2. This shift in power has been especially significant in India. For a long time, governments regarded the country's population as its great liability. Vastly poor and illiterate, India's people were 'the great unwashed,' a burden not just for the country but also a worry for the rest of the world. Today, however, India's growth is credited to its strength in human capital, and the rise of IT in India, for instance, is seen in terms of 'Indian talent,' as entrepreneurs and workers overcame the barriers that existed in the 1990s to drive growth.

3. Our human capital has thus transformed from an albatross into India's most significant advantage. There is a growing realization within our government that India's most critical reforms will be those that impact the quality of our upcoming demographic dividend — and it is consequently policies in education, health, and labour laws that are receiving the closest attention.

4. But the role of people as 'human capital' requires props that are still missing, or only half there. Our vast numbers of people can only participate in our growth story if we provide them 'access' — to the roads that take them to work, to lights that allow them to study at night, and to English skills that enable them to tap into the benefits of our growth.

5. In some ways, the rise of this boom generation is in itself paving the way towards the solutions it needs. The exuberance of this demographic, this pool of restless, ambitious, young workers not hamstrung by tradition and old habit, is a shot in the arm in terms of new ideas and opportunities. And democracy is ensuring that their voices are heard, and the state is beginning to respond.

Answer the following questions:

(a) What does the writer mean by "bit players"? (1)
(b) Describe in your own words the change that has occurred since the 1970s. (2)
(c) How was India's teeming population looked at in the past and how is it now viewed? (2)
(d) What is the 'access' required which will enable our large population of youth to join the growth story? (3)
(e) Describe some of the characteristics of this "boom generation." (2)

2. Vocabulary: (10)

(a) Find words from the reading passage which mean the same as the following: (5)
(i) Something which is regarded as a disadvantage (Paragraph 2)
(ii) Persons who set up businesses (Paragraph 2)
(iii) A very large, chiefly white oceanic bird (Paragraph 3)
(iv) Support structures (Paragraph 4)
(v) Relating to the structure of populations (Paragraph 5)
(b) Find words from the passage which mean the opposite of the following:(5)
(i) Important (Paragraph 1)
(ii) Educated (Paragraph 2)

(iii) Minor (Paragraph 3)
(iv) Demerits (Paragraph 4)
(v) Listlessness (Paragraph 5)

3. Grammar: (10)

(a) Change the following passive sentences into active ones: (5)
(i) Your order has been received by us.
(ii) You have been booked at the Palace Hotel.
(iii) The arrangements for your stay will be made by us.
(iv) You will be received at the airport by our manager.
(v) Our range of garments will certainly be liked by you.

(b) Correct the following sentences: (5)
(i) When you will come to my office?
(ii) Mona is late always.
(iii) We have visited Nainital last summer.
(iv) Sonu is working at this company for the last seven years.
(v) Does many countries have a pollution problem?

4. Write short notes on any two of the following: (10)

(a) It is important to have knowledge of different cultures
(b) Effective group discussions
(c) Basic components of a Business Proposal
(d) Difference between a memo and an office order

5. Report Writing: (10)

A benefactor has given a sum of money to your college. One condition of the gift is that both the students and staff must be involved in deciding how the money is to be used. You have been asked by the Principal of the college to survey the views of staff and students and to present her with an information report. Write a report in 250 words.

BACHELOR OF COMPUTER APPLICATIONS (BCA) (Revised)

Chapter 9: Term-End Examination, December, 2017

BCS-055: BUSINESS COMMUNICATION

Time: 2 Hours
Maximum Marks: 50
Note: Answer all questions.

1. Read the following passage and answer the questions given below: (12)

When a brave mountaineer is assailing the Everest he is as great a hero as a cosmonaut rocketing towards Mars in his space capsule, and thousands of men and women in different countries back his progress with their good wishes and share the thrills and anxieties of his hazardous journey to the roof of the world. Also, scores of anxious scientists wish him success in the hope of obtaining valuable information on atmospheric conditions in the upper regions of the Earth. Mountaineering is indeed a source of pleasure and a mine of useful knowledge which is constantly enriching the scientific vocabulary of geologists, mineralogists, and glaciologists of the world.

Mountaineering is a perennial source of joy to those who have eyes that can appreciate the beauties of nature. Nowhere does nature reveal her charm in greater abundance than on the mountain tops. To lovers of mountains, the sound of waterfalls is like the joyful clapping of merry, primitive dancers, and the howling of night winds contains a musical pleasantness which surpasses the highly sustained rhapsodies of man-made organs. Lakes in high altitudes, holding within their cup-like mountain enclosures the watery wealth of surrounding glaciers, treeless plateaus covered with rare varieties of grass, plants, and flowers, and yawning chasms into whose dark, unfathomable interior nature's countless species of animals and plants carry on their fight for existence, are attractions so powerful and irresistible that no man or woman who is a member of a mountaineering party can turn a deaf ear to their call.

Mountaineering is an awfully risky venture in the case of those ambitious souls who are dreaming of conquering such majestic peaks as Annapurna, Dhaulagiri, and Everest, and who wish to be ranked among the world's greatest climbers, Sir Edmund P. Hillary and Tenzing Norgay. Dozens of adventurers belonging to different nations with their hearts burning with a passion to conquer the highest peak in the world perished in the immortal snows of the Himalayas, after painfully inching their way to heights which were in close proximity to the summit. Expedition after expedition turned back exhausted, frostbitten, and utterly disappointed when the mighty Himalayas hurled icy winds, snowstorms, and blizzards at those who wanted to conquer Everest, thus barring their way to this pinnacle of glory. The bones of many men of unrealized ambition lie buried in the glacial wilderness which is the home of the highest peak in the world. Such awful setbacks, however, did not dampen the enthusiasm of succeeding generations of mountaineers.

Answer the following questions:

(a) Why does the author equate the mountaineer trying to climb Mount Everest to a cosmonaut trying to go to Mars? Give at least two reasons. (2)

(b) 'Mountaineering is a perennial source of joy ... .' Discuss this phrase in the light of the passage. Say for whom, how, and why. (4)

(c) What is the darker side of mountaineering? (3)

(d) Why do you think mountaineers persist in their sport despite mountaineering being such a risky business? (3)

(e) Give a suitable title to the passage. (2)

(f) Would you like to go on a mountaineering trip? Why/Why not? Give reasons. (3)

(g) Make your own sentences with the following phrases from the passage. Pick any three phrases from the five given below: (3)

(i) Hazardous journey
(ii) Mine of useful information
(iii) Perennial source of joy

(iv) In greater abundance
(v) Risky venture

2. Dialogue Writing: (10)
A friend is leaving the country to study abroad. You are part of the organizing team. Discuss with your classmates how best to give him/her a farewell party and a present. Write a dialogue taking about ten turns.

3. Write short notes on any two of the following: (10)
(a) Group Discussions
(b) Safe and Unsafe Topics for Small Talk
(c) Travelling for Business Purposes
(d) Internal Business Reports

4. Fill in the blanks in the following passage with appropriate prepositions: (5)
The Home Minister of Nepal reached Delhi (a) ___ 15th August (b) ___ 10 am. (c) ___ the airport he went (d) ___ Rashtrapati Bhawan. He talked of several developments taking place (e) ___ Nepal and India.

5. Fill in the blanks with the appropriate forms of the verbs in brackets: (5)
(a) Northumbria University ___ (have) a long tradition of welcoming international students.
(b) They ___ (make) special efforts to ensure that everyone ___ (feel) at home.
(c) Their ideal location in Newcastle, and excellent facilities ___ (make) for an enjoyable experience.
(d) Over 200 undergraduate and postgraduate courses ___ (offer) every year.

BACHELOR OF COMPUTER APPLICATIONS (BCA) (Revised)

Chapter 10: Term-End Examination, June, 2018

BCS-055: BUSINESS COMMUNICATION

Time: 2 Hours
Maximum Marks: 50
Note: Answer all questions.

1. Read the following passage and answer the questions given below: (12)

I used to be absolutely petrified of speaking in front of any type of group. In fact, I was so scared that I actually fainted (twice) in high school while attempting to do so. But I'm not alone. I've heard that public speaking is the number one fear in the world. It seems that speaking to groups is even more frightening to people than air travel, bankruptcy, even death!

A fear as big as this one doesn't exist in a vacuum. In other words, it doesn't show up only on those occasions when you are called on to speak in front of a group. Instead, the stress associated with speaking in front of others looms over you, perhaps very subtly, if there is any chance whatsoever that you will ever need to speak in front of people. Whether you may be required to give a presentation, a sales pitch, the results of a report or study, an all-out speech, or simply share an idea with others, the stress factor is the same — enormous — if you're scared.

Another factor to consider is this: If you're frightened of speaking to groups, even a little bit, you may avoid doing things that could greatly benefit your career, give you a promotion or more responsibility, or an advancement of some kind. Before I overcame my fear of speaking, I remember making many decisions based on the likelihood that I may or may not have to speak. Getting over this fear helped me to relax about my work so that I could focus on other things. It made my work life easier and far less stressful. There is no question that overcoming this fear has also helped me to become more successful as an author. Had I not done so, I doubt very much that I would be writing books, because writing books requires promoting them, often in front of huge groups of people.

The way to get over this fear is to put yourself in situations where you are required to speak to groups. You can start really small — even one or two others is a great place to start. There are classes you can take, coaches who can help you, books to read, and tapes to listen to. There are a variety of methods and strategies to look into. In the end, however, you'll have to take the first step and get in front of people. If you do, I think you'll find, as I have, that if you get over this common fear, you'll be richly rewarded in terms of the quality of your work and, indeed, the quality of your life.

Answer the following questions:

(a) What are some of the things that frighten people? What frightened the writer the most? (2)
(b) How does fear of public speaking affect the career of a person? Discuss. (3)
(c) What are the solutions to overcome fear of public speaking? Discuss in the light of the passage. (3)
(d) Talk about your fear of public speaking. What do you do to overcome this fear? (3)
(e) Give a suitable title to the passage. Say why it is appropriate. (2)
(f) Find opposites of the following words from the passage: (3)
(i) Fearless (para 1)
(ii) Obviously (para 2)
(iii) More difficult (para 3)
(g) Make sentences of your own with the following words from the passage: (4)
(i) Show up
(ii) In front of

(iii) Share an idea
(iv) Start really small

2. Dialogue Writing: (10)
Write a dialogue of about 250 words between two friends. The discussion is whether students should take part in politics or not.

3. Write short notes on any two of the following: (10)
(a) Organizing a Portfolio
(b) Phone Interview
(c) Different Types of Communicators
(d) Travelling for Business

4. Fill in the blanks with the appropriate prepositions: (5)
(a) The strain is telling ___ his health.
(b) I saw ___ the trick.
(c) I do not believe ___ what he says.
(d) The father tried to dissuade his son ___ modeling as a career.
(e) He is ineligible ___ this post.

5. Fill in the blanks with can or can't, could or couldn't, may or mayn't, and might or mightn't: (5)
(a) Since I haven't worked throughout the year, I have begun to feel that I ___ pass in the examination.
(b) Thanks for the invitation, Mr. Kapoor. ___ my sister come with me?
(c) Excuse me, I have an urgent phone call to make. ___ I use your telephone?
(d) We could hold the meeting in June, but I think it ___ be the best time. It is too hot then.
(e) You can get to Chandigarh from here, but you ___ get from there to Jaipur.

BACHELOR OF COMPUTER APPLICATIONS (BCA) (Revised)

Chapter 11: Term-End Examination, December, 2018

BCS-055: BUSINESS COMMUNICATION

Time: 2 Hours
Maximum Marks: 50

Note:

Answer all questions.
There are five questions in all.

1. Read the following passage and answer the questions given below: (12)

Already an estimated 50,000 people have tried bungee jumping in the UK alone — and not all of them are crazy!
Some describe it as a close encounter with death; others — the most thrilling experience they've ever had!
So what makes someone bungee jump and what goes through their mind when they're doing it?
Bungee jumping was something I always wanted to do. I saw it as a way of conquering my fear of heights — and that's exactly what it did,' explains experienced jumper Mark Debenham, aged 32.
'50% of people only ever jump once, to prove something to themselves, but many take it up as a sport and jump regularly.'
'Bungee jumping is an amazing experience which leaves your heart racing at up to 170 beats a minute.'
'I've done about 50 jumps, both in this country and abroad, and my highest was from 120 metres.'
'My first ever jump was extremely frightening. The next seven or eight jumps were still very scary but then after that it was pure excitement.'
'When you actually jump you seriously think you're going to die. It doesn't matter how many people you see jump before you, your mind tells you, you shouldn't be doing it.'
'It takes about four or five seconds before the rope snaps you back up again, giving you a momentary feeling of weightlessness. It's then you realise you've survived the jump and at that point most people let out a yell of relief.'
'I've done quite a few different styles of jumping. You can jump forwards, backwards, somersault or jump with someone else.'
People think of bungee jumping as being dangerous, but in reality it's extremely safe, and injuries are rare.'
'I have a lot of confidence in the equipment and I just enjoy jumping.'
You have to be over 14 years of age. If you're 50 or more you need to have a medical certificate. There are also various other medical conditions which prevent you from doing a jump. A qualified instructor can guide you on these.
It is important that you only jump with a licensed club which is fully insured.

Answer the following questions:

(i) What are the different reactions of people who have tried bungee jumping? (2)
(ii) Why do people bungee jump? Give two reasons from the passage. (2)
(iii) If people jump once, do they usually try it again? Give instance(s) from the passage. (2)
(iv) Describe the feeling of a person before the jump. (2)
(v) How does the person feel just after the jump? (2)
(b) Make a sentence with each of the following words taken from the passage: (5)
(i) Extremely
(ii) Encounter
(iii) Scary
(iv) Yell
(v) Momentary

(c) Find words from the passage which mean the opposite of the following: (5)
(i) Normal
(ii) Mundane
(iii) Rarely
(iv) Lowest
(v) Safe

2. Fill in the blanks with suitable forms of the verbs given in the box: (5)

read, have, do, leave, bring
(a) Every time uncle Rohit comes to see us, he ___ us a present.
(b) Haven't you finished the book yet? You ___ it for ages.
(c) He can't answer his phone now, he ___ his 'keep-fit' exercises.
(d) It began to get very cold. Unfortunately, we ___ our coats at home.
(e) I love this necklace, I've ___ it for nearly thirty years.

3. Change the following sentences from active voice to passive voice: (5)

(a) They presented the winners with gold medals.
(b) They're going to pierce my ears this afternoon.
(c) Someone should have told us about the incident.
(d) Your rooms have been booked for two days at the Mountain hotel.
(e) You will be received at the railway station by the hotel taxi.

4. Write short notes on any two of the following: (10)

(a) Building workplace relationships through small talk
(b) Preparing to face an interview
(c) E-mail etiquette
(d) Planning a business event

5. Write a profile of yourself: (10)

Use the following points. You may add some more. The profile must be in about 200 words.

1. Current job
2. Responsibilities you are required to undertake
3. Skills required to fulfill these responsibilities
4. Brief outline of previous job and skills developed during that period
5. Educational qualifications
6. Career path you would like to chart out.

You may write in any order you like.

BACHELOR OF COMPUTER APPLICATIONS (BCA) (Revised)

Chapter 12: Term-End Examination, June, 2019

BCS-055: BUSINESS COMMUNICATION

Time: 2 Hours
Maximum Marks: 50
Note: Answer all five questions.

1. Read the following passage and answer the questions given below: (20)

I don't think most people realize how stressful it can be to have multiple incomplete tasks hanging over your head. Just in case you are one of these people, let me assure you, it is stressful. I like to call this the "almost finished syndrome." It has always intrigued me because often, it would be relatively easy to simply bear down and complete something — not almost complete something, but really complete it 100 percent, and get it out of the way.

On many occasions, I've hired people for everything from a building or repair project around the house to an editing job at work. The person I've hired has been competent, creative, hard-working, skilled, and motivated. Yet for some strange reason, they won't quite finish the job. Sure, they almost finish — sometimes they are about 99 percent done, but that last remaining bit seems to hang over their heads (and mine too). Often the last 1 percent takes as long as the first 99 percent.

When you absolutely finish a project, several good things happen. First, you enjoy the nice feeling of a sense of completion. It feels good knowing you've set out to do something and it's done, it's out of the way. Completion allows you to move forward without the distraction of having things hanging over your head.

Beyond the obvious, however, is the respect you feel for yourself and the respect you secure from others when you complete something. You said you were going to do something, and you did it — all of it. You send the message to others that "I am a person of my word," "You can trust me," and "I am reliable." And you affirm the message to yourself: "I am competent and trustworthy." This makes people want to help you — and want to refer business to you and want you to succeed.

Whether you are working for a corporation or a customer, it's undeniable that people will be irritated at you if you don't complete your tasks as agreed. Further, they will be on your back, complaining to you and about you. How can this be worth the stress it so obviously creates? Wouldn't it be easier to simply plan ahead and do whatever is necessary to get the job done — all the way done?

This is an easy habit to break. Take an honest look at your own tendencies. If you are someone who often almost finishes something, take note of the tendency and commit yourself to that last final completion. You can do it — and when you do, your life is going to seem so much easier.

Answer the following questions:

(i) What does the author mean by the phrase "almost finished syndrome"? (2)
(ii) Describe the feelings of yourself and others when you complete a project. (Give four examples). (4)
(iii) What is the reaction of customers or a corporation when you leave things incomplete? (2)
(iv) Give a suitable title to the passage. Give reasons. (2)
(b) Make a sentence each with the following words/phrases from the passage: (5)
(i) Stressful
(ii) Occasions
(iii) Motivated
(iv) Sense of completion
(v) Reliable
(c) Find words from the passage which are the opposite of the following: (5)
(i) Peaceful
(ii) Difficult
(iii) Incapable

(iv) Fail
(v) Praising

2. Fill in the blanks with the verbs given in the brackets: (5)

There ___ (be) a car by the side of the road. It ___ (broke) down and the driver ___ (try) to repair it. So, we ___ (stop) by to see if we ___ (can) help.

3. Fill in the blanks with appropriate articles (*a, an, the*): (5)

(a) In essence, strike out for ___ middle path between over-confidence and timidity.
(b) Entertain healthy respect both for ___ people you work with and yourself.
(c) How do you get noticed when you're working as part of ___ team, and are expected to blend seamlessly with ___ rest?

4. Write short notes on any two of the following: (10)

(a) Writing an effective CV
(b) Communicating across cultures
(c) Features of a good proposal
(d) Difference between a resume and a portfolio

5. Dialogue Writing: (10)

Your company owns a small field next to the factory. You will probably need it in a year or so if you extend the factory. What can you do with it in the meantime? Write a dialogue in about 150–200 words, discussing the issue with your boss.

BACHELOR OF COMPUTER APPLICATIONS (BCA) (Revised)

Chapter 13: Term-End Examination, December, 2019

BCS-055: BUSINESS COMMUNICATION

Time: 2 Hours
Maximum Marks: 50
Note: Answer all questions.

1. Read the following passage and answer the questions given below: (20)

TOKYO—A recent television special said it all: It showed a building in downtown Tokyo with pre-programmed office lights that uniformly shut off at 10 p.m.; seconds later, virtually every light in the building came right back on. Despite such displays, the nation that has taken the sting out of the word 'workaholic', producing 10 percent of the world's exports with just 2 percent of its population, is suddenly obsessed with a deadly phenomenon known as karoshi. That's the Japanese word for 'death from overwork.' Tetsunojo Uehata, the medical authority who coined the word, defines karoshi as a 'condition in which psychologically unsound work processes are allowed to continue in a way that disrupts the worker's normal work and life rhythms, leading to a buildup of fatigue in the body and a chronic condition of overwork accompanied by a worsening of preexistent high blood pressure and a hardening of the arteries and finally resulting in a fatal breakdown.' Translation: All work and no play can really wreck one's health, even in Japan.

Hardly a week goes by without a grim report about some overzealous worker in the prime of his life who could not just say no to overtime. Not long ago, a 39-year-old police sergeant, Haruo Okada, captured headlines as a karoshi victim by working double shifts for a month during the enthronement ceremonies for the nation's new monarch. There are no reliable figures on the number of victims, but analysts believe that tens of thousands of Japanese become seriously ill or die from overwork each year. Despite promises by the government to trim working hours, the average Japanese worker clocked 2,150 hours in 1989, compared with 1,924 hours for Americans and 1,634 hours for the French.

Some Japanese want change. When a group of lawyers and doctors set up the nation's first karoshi hotline in 1988, 135 people phoned in on the first day. Since then, nearly 2,000 cases have been reported to the 42 hotlines across the nation, and an international call-in center has been set up recently.

To raise public awareness about the problem and to pressure the government and corporate Japan into action, a group of lawyers, doctors, and victims' wives has published a book called "Karoshi: When the Corporate Warrior Dies," which recounts numerous horror stories. Yet the government and most Japanese companies rarely acknowledge karoshi and provide no special compensation to survivors. As the Ministry of Labour defines it, overwork can only be considered a cause of death if a victim "worked continuously for 24 hours preceding death," or "worked 16 hours a day for several consecutive days leading up to death."

Alas, the recent media attention probably won't slow down the production lines much. In a poll conducted by an insurance company, more than 40 percent of the employees the firm covered said they feared that overwork might kill them; few planned to do anything about it. All in all, it looks like another busy year for the folks at the karoshi hotline.

Answer the following questions:

(i) Why did "virtually every light in the building come right back on"? What does this tell you about the Japanese people? (2)

(ii) Write in your own words what the word "karoshi" means. Do you have such a word in your language? (2)

(iii) Why does the Japanese Government need to "trim" the working hours of its employees? (2)

(iv) The government and most Japanese companies rarely acknowledge "karoshi." Why? (2)

(v) Give a suitable title to the passage. (2)

(b) State whether the following statements are true or false: (5)
(i) Most Japanese people compulsively work very hard.
(ii) Most Japanese have deep-rooted psychological problems.
(iii) The government of Japan is concerned but helpless about the situation.
(iv) The lights in the office building are shut off by the workers.
(v) About 40% of Japanese know that they will die from overwork.

(c) Make sentences with each of the following words (the sentences must not be copied from the passage): (5)
(i) Shut off
(ii) Workaholic
(iii) Disrupts
(iv) Victim
(v) Compensation

2. Memo Writing: (10)

At the place where you work, too many people leave without permission and do not account for it later. You are the office manager. Write a memo to the employees to address this issue.

3. Write short notes on any two of the following: (10)

(i) Business Event Planning
(ii) Features of a Proposal
(iii) Writing a CV
(iv) Group Discussion

4. Rewrite the following sentences using the passive form: (5)

(i) People won't obey the rules unless you enforce them.
(ii) Someone should have told us.
(iii) They are going to pierce our ears this afternoon.
(iv) They presented the winners with gold medals.
(v) I am sure someone was following me.

5. Fill in the blanks with the appropriate form of the verbs given in brackets: (5)

(i) My parents ___ (give) me a teddy bear for my third birthday.
(ii) If you ask her nicely, she ___ (give) it back to you.
(iii) Haven't you finished the book yet? You ___ (read) it for ages.
(iv) I ___ (read) three of his novels already.
(v) You won't see me tomorrow, I ___ (leave) very early tomorrow.

BACHELOR OF COMPUTER APPLICATIONS (BCA) (Revised)

Chapter 14: Term-End Examination, June, 2020

BCS-055: BUSINESS COMMUNICATION

Time: 2 Hours
Maximum Marks: 50
Note: Answer all five questions.

1. Read the following passage and answer the questions given below: (20)

The important thing is not where you were or where you are but where you want to get.

The progressive corporation plans company goals 10 to 15 years ahead. Executives who manage leading businesses must ask, "Where do we want our company to be 10 years from now?" Then they gauge their efforts accordingly. New plant capacity is built not for today's needs but rather for needs 5 to 10 years in the future. Research is undertaken to develop products which won't appear for a decade or longer.

The modern corporation does not leave its future to chance. Should you?

Each of us can learn a precious lesson from the forward-looking business. We can and should plan at least 10 years ahead. You must form an image now of the person you want to be 10 years from now if you are to become that image. This is a critical thought. Just as the business that neglects to plan ahead will be just another business (if it even survives), the individual that fails to set long-range goals will most certainly be just another person lost in life's shuffle. Without goals, we cannot grow.

Let me share with you an example of why we must have long-run goals to achieve real success. Just last week a young man (let me call him F. B.) came to me with a career problem. F. B. looked well-mannered and intelligent. He was single and had finished college four years ago.

We talked for a while about what he was doing now, his education, his aptitudes, and general background. Then I said to him, "You came to see me for help on making a job change. What kind of job are you looking for?"

"Well," he said, "that's what I came to see you about. I don't know what I want to do."

His problem, of course, was a very common one. But I realized that just to arrange for the young man to have interviews with several possible employers would not help him. Trial and error is a pretty poor way to select a career. With dozens of career possibilities, odds of stumbling into the right choice are several dozen to one.

Answer the following questions:

(i) In the context of the passage, explain the first line of the passage: "The important thing is not where you were or where you are but where you want to get." (3)
(ii) Why do progressive corporations plan company goals 10 to 15 years ahead? Discuss in the light of the passage. (2)
(iii) What is the "critical thought" which the writer is referring to? (2)
(iv) What do you understand about the character of F. B.? (2)
(v) Give a suitable title to the passage. (1)

(b) Make a sentence with each of the following words/phrases from the passage: (5)
(i) Gauge
(ii) Undertaken
(iii) Image
(iv) Aptitude
(v) Stumbling

(c) Find words from the passage which are the opposite of the following: (5)
(i) Backward
(ii) Old-fashioned
(iii) Dies
(iv) Failure
(v) Dull

2. Complete the text with the correct form of the verb in brackets: (5)

Sunil Sethis ___ (be) at Ultra Tech Inc. since he ___ (leave) college. Since he ___ (join) the company, he ___ (work) in three different departments. In his present job in the Sales Department, he ___ (travel) to Spain every two or three months.

3. Complete the following sentences using *must*, *mustn't*, or *needn't*: (5)

(i) I've got an important meeting tomorrow, I ___ be late.

(ii) I haven't got any money left, I ___ go to the ATM.

(iii) The restaurant is never full. We ___ book in advance.

(iv) We've got plenty of time, we ___ hurry.

(v) Please check this letter carefully. There ___ be any mistakes.

4. Dialogue Writing: (10)

Your company has recently established a 'friendly coworker' programme in which employees are assigned to orient new employees to the company. You are part of this programme. Write a dialogue that you have with a new employee who has joined the marketing team. Introduce her to the manager and explain to her the policies of the company. Write the dialogue in about 150 to 200 words.

5. Write short notes on any two of the following: (10)

(i) Social small talk in business

(ii) The importance of Group Discussions

(iii) The difference between a memo and a business letter

(iv) Understanding other cultures is important in business

BACHELOR OF COMPUTER APPLICATIONS (BCA) (Revised)
Chapter 15: Term-End Examination, February, 2021
BCS-055: BUSINESS COMMUNICATION

Time: 2 Hours
Maximum Marks: 50
Note: Answer all five questions.

1. Read the following passage and answer the questions given below: (20)
Dr. Collett suggests that if we compare the way different European nations use gestures, they fall into three groups. In the first group are the Nordic nations — the Swedes, Finns, Norwegians, and Danes — who use gestures very little. The second group includes nations such as the British, Germans, Dutch, Belgians, and Russians. They use some gestures, for example, when they are excited, or want to communicate over long distances, or to insult each other. The third group includes the Italians, Greeks, French, Spanish, and Portuguese. They use gestures a lot, to emphasize what they are saying, and to hold the other person's attention. 'Even when they are silent,' says Dr. Collett, 'their hands are often busy sending messages through the medium of manual semaphore.'

Personal space
People's sense of 'personal space' — the distance that separates them from another person — also varies between people of different nationalities. What feels right for one nationality may feel uncomfortable for another. British zoologist, Desmond Morris, has identified three 'personal space' zones in Europe. In countries such as Spain, France, Italy, and Greece, people stand close enough to touch each other easily. Morris calls this the 'elbow zone'. In East European countries such as Poland, Hungary, and Romania, people stand a little more distant. Morris calls this the 'wrist zone' because they are close enough to touch wrists. In Britain, Holland, Belgium, Germany, and the Scandinavian countries, people prefer to stand further away from each other, and they do not generally touch. This he calls the 'fingertips zone.'

Eye contact
Another cultural difference between nationalities is the amount of eye contact between people. In countries where people stand close to each other, in Morris's elbow zone, eye contact is more frequent and lasts longer. Mediterranean countries, says Dr. Collett, are 'high-look' cultures whereas north European countries are 'low-look' cultures. Children who grow up in low-look cultures learn that it is rude to look too long at another person. In a high-look culture, eye contact, like physical contact and gestures, is a natural way of expressing your feelings and relating to other people. This explains why, for example, north Europeans visiting south European countries may feel uncomfortable at the way people look at them.

Answer the following questions:
(i) Which nationalities in Europe usually use
  a. lots of gestures when they speak?
  b. very few gestures when they speak?(2)
(ii) In a conversation, why might a north European move away from, and a South European move closer to, the person they are talking to? (2)
(iii) Why might north Europeans visiting Mediterranean countries feel uncomfortable at the way people look at them? (2)
(iv) Understanding the 'body language' of different nationalities is important in the business context. Discuss. (2)
(v) Give a title to the passage. Discuss why you chose the title. (2)
(b) Make a sentence each with the following words/phrases from the passage: (5)
(i) Gestures
(ii) Excited

(iii) Personal space
(iv) Eye contact
(v) Rude
(c) Find words from the passage which are the opposite of the following: (5)
(i) Appreciate
(ii) Noisy
(iii) Far
(iv) Rare
(v) Polite

2. Fill in the blanks with the correct forms of the verbs given in brackets: (5)

In her career, Ms. Paramvir ___ (travel) widely in Europe, the USA, and the Far East. She ___ (make) many useful contacts in these countries. Her professional experience ___ (give) her a wide knowledge of the luxury holiday market. However, she ___ (never, travel) on a luxury train, but she ___ (travel) across China by an ordinary train when she was a student.

3. Complete the following sentences: (5)

(i) People would be healthier if ___.
(ii) If we banned cars in city centres, ___.
(iii) The air in our cities would be cleaner if ___.
(iv) If public transport were free ___.
(v) People wouldn't use their cars so much in cities if ___.

4. Write short notes on any two of the following, giving examples where necessary:(10)

(a) Setting up a business event
(b) Features of a memo
(c) Preparing to face an interview
(d) Characteristics of a business report

5. Assume that you have selected a company that you want to work for and the position you want to be hired for. Then answer this question:

Why should this employer hire you for this job? Give as many reasons as you can in a paragraph of 250 words. (10)

BACHELOR OF COMPUTER APPLICATIONS (BCA) (Revised)

Chapter 16: Term-End Examination, June, 2021

BCS-055: BUSINESS COMMUNICATION

Time: 2 Hours
Maximum Marks: 50
Note: Answer all five questions.

1. Read the following passage and answer the questions that follow: (20)

Problem solving is wrestling with algebra or chemistry homework. But it's also taking on the day-to-day challenges of being a human being. At school or work, you are confronted by challenging situations. For example, what do you do about a lost wallet, a misunderstanding with a friend or co-worker, or a forgotten assignment? How well and how quickly you deal with these situations matters. Your problem-solving skills can greatly influence your personal and professional success.

A + Appeal

The ability to solve problems efficiently is one of the top 10 qualities that companies want in new employees. This is what Kellah M. Edens says. She is an education professor at the University of South Carolina in Columbia. "During job interviews, it's common to be asked 'what if' questions," says Edens. "How you answer will demonstrate your problem-solving ability. Generally, these questions deal with real problems in the workplace."

Why do interviewers ask "what if" questions? Applicants with good problem-solving skills usually have positive personality traits, such as patience, independence, and curiosity. Good problem solvers usually have self-esteem, competence, and a responsible attitude toward decision-making. "Other problem-solving traits include flexibility, open-mindedness, and tolerance for ambiguity (uncertainty)," says Edens.

Step-by-Step

The most productive problem solvers are also creative. Take Albert Einstein. The world-famous physicist understood that most problems have many possible answers. And the first answer is not always the best. Generating multiple solutions is highly desirable. To do this, you must think less rigidly, or 'outside the box,' says Michael Michalko, author of *Thinkertoys: A Handbook of Business Creativity.*

Evaluate each alternative. Don't criticize yourself or feel embarrassed by any errors you make, writes Michael E. Martinez, an education professor at the University of California at Irvine. If one real-life exercise doesn't get the hoped-for result, try another and another. Remain coolheaded. "Allow enough time for ideas to form," suggests Edens.

How do you do that? Take a step-by-step approach to problem-solving.

(I) State the problem in the form of a question. Make it clear and specific.
(II) Gather accurate information.
(III) Brainstorm a wide variety of solutions, both creative and conventional.
(IV) Examine and try alternatives.
(V) Choose a solution.

Answer the following questions:

(i) Why is it important to develop problem-solving skills? (2)
(ii) Why do you think employers ask 'what if' questions during a job interview? (2)
(iii) What traits do good problem solvers have? Why are they important? (2)
(iv) How do you think Albert Einstein tried to solve problems? Why? (2)
(v) What must you do to generate multiple solutions? What two things shouldn't you do? (4)
(vi) Make sentences with the following words/phrases in your own words. Do not copy from the passage: (8)

wrestling with, confronted by, deal with, demonstrate, curiosity, self-esteem, out-of-the-box, coolheaded

2. Letter Writing: (10)

The students in your study centre do not have a place to meet or relax before or after class. Your centre has an extra room, but it is old and dirty without chairs and tables. You want to turn this space into a 'student room'. Write a letter to the head of the study centre, persuading him/her to agree to your ideas. Describe in detail what you want implemented. Give some suggestions on how this might be done.

3. Write short notes on any two of the following: (5 each)

(i) Walk-in interviews

(ii) The importance of small-talk in business encounters

(iii) Features of a proposal

(iv) Communicating across cultures

4. Fill in the blanks: (5)

Complete their answers with the comparative or superlative form of the adjective/adverb in brackets:

(i) For me the ___ (bad) thing is walking along the street with a boy who's constantly looking at his reflection in shop windows because he thinks he's the ___ (good-looking) person in the world.

(ii) There's nothing ___ (irritating) than trying to tie a shoelace when one end is much ___ (short) than the other.

(iii) For me the ___ (annoying) thing is sitting next to a person with headphones on a bus, moving his head with the music.

5. Change the following sentences into passive voice: (5)

(i) He may win the prize.

(ii) The doctor was examining the patient.

(iii) We must respect our elders.

(iv) They built a new bridge over the river.

(v) A team of experts is preparing the report.

BACHELOR OF COMPUTER APPLICATIONS (BCA) (Revised)

Chapter 17: Term-End Examination, December, 2021

BCS-055: BUSINESS COMMUNICATION

Time: 2 Hours
Maximum Marks: 50
Note: Answer all questions.

1. Read the following passage and answer the questions given below: (20)

Passage

Silence is the absence of oral communication and may have some body signals, gestures, facial expressions, etc., associated with it. This is perhaps a very passive non-verbal medium, but it can become an effective communicative tool. The very absence of words allows the receiver to concentrate on other cues. When a person becomes silent, that in itself sends a message, and usually, silence communicates the mental status. Giving utterance to mental state is not only difficult but, at times, even undesirable. Silence is an effective tool for these moments. As the person becomes silent, he provides himself an opportunity for mental relaxation, as also gathering and organizing his thoughts.

Because it is a passive medium, silence also has the potential of being interpreted as a sign of suffering from fear or being respectful. But in the absence of verbal clarifications, the interpretation of silence could be wide. It can be shyness or disgust or sadness that prompts people to silence, and it may not be an easy task to unravel its mystery. Misunderstanding silence is also common. People may read something totally off the mark in another person's silence.

Communicators, however, need to use silence, keeping in mind some of its limitations. One of the main limitations is that silence is often taken for assent, and it is difficult to express disagreement through it. In meetings and group activities, silence may rob the group of a member's viewpoint (that is, the primary cause of his presence). Remaining silent in such a setting may send out wrong signals: that either the person is not interested or that he is ignorant about the issues being discussed.

Answer the following questions:

(a) What are the body signals that help people interpret silence? (2)
(b) What is the ''message'' that silence sends in a business context? (2)
(c) ''The interpretation of silence could be wide.'' Discuss in the light of the passage. (3)
(d) What are the limitations of keeping silent? (3)
(e) Find opposites of the following words from the passage: (5)
   (i) presence (para 1)
   (ii) tension (para 1)
   (iii) narrow (para 2)
   (iv) advantages (para 3)
   (v) knowledgeable (para 3)
(f) Make sentences of your own with the following words/phrases from the passage:(5)
   (i) gestures
   (ii) cues
   (iii) off the mark
   (iv) assent
   (v) send out wrong signals

2. Write a composition in about 250 words on any one of the following: (10)

(a) My first day at work
(b) Why I chose my present career?

(c) The work/profession that I would enjoy
(d) The difficulties experienced in doing a particular job

3. Write short notes on any two of the following: (10)

(a) The importance of small talk in business communication
(b) The different styles of communication
(c) Features of a memo
(d) A good interview

4. Complete the following with the appropriate form of the verb given in brackets: (5)

(a) You must never _________ (open) the door to a stranger.
(b) He is _________ (look) forward to his annual vacation.
(c) I _________ (see) the Qutub Minar last year.
(d) Although I _________ (try) very hard, I did not succeed.
(e) Every year, on his birthday, he _________ (host) a grand party for family and friends.

5. Change the following into passive voice: (5)

(a) We must not disobey the rules of the organisation.
(b) Nature has given us many treasures.
(c) Exercise can prevent many diseases.
(d) America made use of the first atom bomb.
(e) Virat Kohli has scored many sixes in his career.

BACHELOR OF COMPUTER APPLICATIONS (BCA) (Revised)

Chapter 18: Term-End Examination, June, 2022

BCS-055: BUSINESS COMMUNICATION

Time: 2 Hours
Maximum Marks: 50
Note: Answer all questions.

1. Read the following passage and answer the questions given below: (20)

Passage

Relationships with colleagues is probably one of the most difficult problems with which the junior worker is faced. For one thing, there is always a certain element of competition between staff for promotion, and this can lead to all kinds of suspicion of the motives of fellow workers. The ambitious drive of some people can make them very difficult to work with. It can be very disturbing, for example, to discover that one's mistakes are being relayed to the 'higher-ups' by colleagues who are seeking to benefit themselves by that method. Unfortunately, human nature being what it is, this kind of situation does happen, and when it is discovered, the relationships within an organisation can be seriously impaired. This is not an easy situation to deal with because there is little defence against an accusation which is justifiable. The fact that we are all prone to error is no real defence. What irritates and frustrates us the most is that we have been betrayed by those with whom we work, and once the resentment and suspicion get to work, our 'communicability' is lessened because we become more guarded and less than frank with our colleagues. Perhaps we should look at a couple of the main motives which make the promotion seeker what he is.

The first motive, not unnaturally, is the desire to earn more money. Most of us never seem to have enough money anyway, and it is not unreasonable to want more. The age we live in places a high value on the possession of money and what it can buy, so the urge to increase our income is very strong in most of us.

The second motive behind promotion seeking is what we loosely call 'status'. This is closely linked with money, of course, but is based on the belief that the higher up the ladder we climb, the more we receive the satisfactions of respect and authority. We may certainly acquire a measure of power and authority, but respect is another matter. Respect depends more on the nature and personality of a person than on his position in an organisation.

It is important to recognise the efforts, even among junior staff, to acquire both money and status and to be aware of the kind of threat they create to human relationships at this level.

Answer the following questions:

(a) Suggest two difficulties that junior workers face in their relationships with colleagues. (2)
(b) When is our 'communicability' lessened at the workplace and why? (3)
(c) What are the motives that drive a promotion seeker? (2)
(d) What does the writer mean when he says "respect is another matter"? (2)
(e) Give a suitable title to the passage. (1)
(f) Give opposites of the following words from the passage: (4)
   (i) disturbing
   (ii) frank
   (iii) increase
   (iv) strong
(g) Make sentences with the following words/phrases from the text: (6)
   (i) suspicion
   (ii) ambitious drive
   (iii) impaired
   (iv) high value

(v) status
(vi) personality

2. There has been a fire in your office. Write a report in about 250 words on: (10)

– How it started
– Any casualties/injuries
– How it was put out
– What steps to prevent further occurrences

3. Write short notes on any two of the following: (10)

(a) Planning an event
(b) Travelling for business
(c) The importance of small talk in business
(d) Dealing with problem letters

4. Fill in the blanks with appropriate linkers in the box: (5)

but, besides, in addition, as well, and, either, moreover

(a) __________ to shorthand, she is qualified in bookkeeping.
(b) The new job pays a higher salary __________ being closer to home.
(c) The manager wasn't fair and he wasn't honest __________.
(d) He told me the reason why he left __________ many more things.
(e) He lost half a fortune, __________ he managed to save his life.

5. Fill in the blanks with appropriate form of the verbs given in brackets: (5)

(a) When we __________ (read) about the Titanic, the story was not new to me because I __________ (see) the movie.
(b) When the Titanic __________ (leave) England, many of the lifeboats __________ (passive: remove).
(c) When the Titanic sank, a rescue ship __________ (come) to pick up the survivors.

BACHELOR OF COMPUTER APPLICATIONS (BCA) (Revised)

Chapter 19: Term-End Examination, December, 2022

BCS-055: BUSINESS COMMUNICATION

Time: 2 Hours
Maximum Marks: 50
Note: Answer all questions.

1. Read the following passage and answer the questions given below: (20)

Passage

To me, there are very few human qualities less appealing than someone who is highly self-absorbed. A person who falls into this category takes him or herself extremely seriously. They love to listen to themselves speak, and value their own time—but no one else's. They are usually quite selfish with their time, love, and money, in addition to lacking compassion for those less fortunate. They are arrogant and come across as pompous and self-righteous. Self-absorbed individuals see others and often treat others as instruments or objects to get something they want. They usually see only one point of view—their own. They are right, and everyone else is wrong, unless, of course, you agree with them.

People who are self-absorbed can be rude, insensitive to the feelings of others, and primarily interested in themselves—their own wants, needs, and desires. They tend to see people in a hierarchical manner. In other words, they see certain people as being beneath them and, as such, they see them as less important than they are. Finally, self-absorbed people are poor listeners because, quite frankly, they aren't very interested in other people beyond a superficial level.

Obviously, I'm painting a worst-case scenario picture. Very few people are quite this bad. I paint this picture, however, because I believe it's important to be fully aware of what type of person you absolutely never, under any set of circumstances, want to become. This encourages you to be certain that none of these ugly characteristics ever creep into your life, and if they do, that you act quickly to move in a different direction.

Don't confuse self-esteem with self-absorption. The two are completely unrelated. In fact, you could say that the two are virtually opposite in nature. A person with high self-esteem loves others and feels good about herself. Because she already has what she needs in an emotional sense (feeling positive about herself), her natural instinct is to reach out to others in an unselfish way. She's extremely interested in hearing what other people have to say and in learning from them. She's very compassionate, always looking for ways to be of service or ways to be kind and generous. She is humble and treats everyone with respect and kindness.

There are many excellent reasons to become less self-absorbed. To begin with, as you can see by the picture I have painted, being self-absorbed is an ugly human quality. Beyond that, being self-absorbed is highly stressful. In fact, self-absorbed people sweat the small stuff as much, or more, than any other group of people—everything bothers or frustrates them. It seems that nothing is ever good enough.

For instance, self-absorbed people often have very poor learning curves. Since they don't listen well and aren't interested in other people, they don't have the advantage of learning from them. In addition, self-absorption comes across loud and clear to others, making them extremely resistant to wanting to be supportive or of any significant help. It's difficult to cheer on an arrogant person. In fact, it's tempting to want to see them fail.

(a) Answer the following questions:

(i) List four qualities of highly self-absorbed people. (2)

(ii) What do you think the writer means by the phrase "they tend to see people in a hierarchical manner"? (2)

(iii) What, according to the writer, is the difference between a self-absorbed person and a person who has

self-esteem? (2)
(iv) Why are self-absorbed people highly stressed? (2)
(v) Why do you think self-absorbed people are unlikely to succeed? (2)

(b) Pick out words from the passage which mean the same as the following words/phrases: (5)

(i) Sympathy and consideration (para 1)
(ii) Having a sense of self-importance (para 1)
(iii) Pride and faith in oneself (para 4)
(iv) Makes them energy and disheartened (para 5)
(v) Proud and conceited person (para 6)

(c) Make sentences of your own with each of the following words from the passage: (5)

(i) Point of view
(ii) Superficial
(iii) Creep into your life
(iv) Supportive
(v) Humble

2. Write short notes on any two of the following: (10)

(i) Preparing for an interview
(ii) The importance of small talk in business
(iii) Organising oneself for business travel
(iv) Different styles and types of communicators
(v) Types of internal communication

3. (a) Fill in the blanks with appropriate conjunctions in the sentences given below: (5)
if, in case, unless, until, when

(i) We are unable to supply the goods __________ we receive payment in advance.
(ii) A spare axle is provided __________ one is damaged during routine use.
(iii) The machine should not be modified __________ a service engineer is present.
(iv) The filter should be changed __________ the unit has been in operation for two months.
(v) The red light will come on __________ the machine overheats.

(b) Rewrite the sentences in the passive voice:
(5)

(i) Somebody cleans the office every day.
(ii) They canceled all flights because of the fog.
(iii) How do people learn languages?
(iv) People don't use this road very often.
(v) They have built a new hospital near the airport.

4. Make a short presentation using about ten slides on any one of the following topics: (10)

(i) An industry that interests you
(ii) Changes that you would like at your workplace

BACHELOR OF COMPUTER APPLICATIONS (BCA) (Revised)

Chapter 20: Term-End Examination, June, 2023

BCS-055: BUSINESS COMMUNICATION

Time: 2 Hours
Maximum Marks: 50
Note: Answer all questions.
1. Read the following passage and answer the questions given below: (20)
Passage:

Whether you are leading a team at work, captaining your local sports team, or in charge of a major company, your style of leadership is a critical factor in the success of your team. So what makes an effective leader? According to Professor D. Quinn Mills of the Harvard Business School, research shows that there are certain preferred leadership qualities that are common to all cultures.

In general, people appreciate leaders who appear honest and trustworthy. However, integrity is a complex idea, often determined by national culture, and what is considered honest in one society is not necessarily so in another. Convection—a strong belief in what you are doing—is a characteristic of leaders in all cultures, but how it is displayed can vary widely. Demonstrating a wholehearted commitment to the success of your team or project is possibly more overt in America than elsewhere. However, a passionate leader with energy and enthusiasm—someone who can energize and inspire their team to succeed—is an asset almost everywhere. Similarly, in most cultures, it helps to be a good communicator, to be people-focused, and to have well-developed interpersonal skills.

The ability to make good decisions quickly is something most cultures see as important. However, being decisive means different things to different people. European and Japanese leaders are the most collaborative decision-makers, taking time to consult with colleagues and consider the options. This is typical of a more participative style of leadership. In contrast, Chinese leaders, for whom the typical role model is often the head of the family, are more likely to make decisions personally. This more autocratic approach tends to be typical of task-oriented, top-down leaders, where what counts is results—it is also frequent in American leaders.

Being adaptable is also an important quality; team leaders often need to be flexible in their response to changing circumstances. Similarly, the ability to delegate and to know when to be hands-off is also necessary.

There's evidence that being able to show empathy—to understand the feelings, needs, and motivation of others—is increasingly seen as a key trait of effective leadership in the United States and Europe, and will become more important in Asia as companies have to compete for managerial talent in a global market. Related to this, certain Asian cultures value leaders who are self-aware and humble—the ability to know yourself and accept your limitations is often a trait of the most effective leaders.

(a) Answer the questions given below:

(i) How do leaders show empathy? Why would this trait become more important in Asian companies? (2)
(ii) What is the difference in leadership style between the economies of Western Europe and Japan and that of China? (2)
(iii) Why is 'integrity' a complex idea? (2)
(iv) What trait is especially valued in certain Asian cultures? (2)
(v) Give a title to this passage and say why you think it is appropriate. (2)

(b) Pick out words from the text which mean the same as the following: (5)

(i) Crucial (Para 1)
(ii) The quality of being honest (Para 2)
(iii) Done in an open way, not secretly (Para 3)

(iv) Demanding that people obey completely (Para 4)
(v) Quality (Para 6)

(c) Make sentences of your own with the following words: (5)

(i) Appreciate
(ii) Displayed
(iii) People-focused
(iv) Collaborative
(v) Flexible

2. Write short notes on any two of the following: (10)

(i) Characteristics of a report
(ii) Differences between written and oral communication
(iii) The importance of culture in business communication
(iv) Organizing a portfolio
(v) Characteristics of a group discussion

3. (a) Fill in the blanks with appropriate verbs given in the brackets: (5)

(i) The night our mother ______ (go) to the shop and ______ (do not) come back. What ______ (happen)? I don't know.
(ii) I ______ (buy) a new car last month, but I ______ (not sell) my old car yet, so at the moment I have two cars.

(b) Change the following sentences into the passive voice: (5)

(i) The cook is tasting the soup.
(ii) Anu answered all the questions easily.
(iii) Rina lost her passport.
(iv) You cannot park the car here.
(v) Who broke the chair?

4. As a secretary of a sports club, write a letter of about 150 words to a secretary of a similar club to explore the possibility of arranging matches or contests (especially sports) between the members of your respective clubs next season. It may be useful to refer to the situation and amenities of your sports ground. (10)

© Author and Publisher 2024

Printed at Repro India Ltd.